Franklin D. Roosevelt

A Great Leader in Troubled Times

Lisa Perlman Greathouse

Consultant

Jennifer M. Lopez, NBCT, M.S.Ed.
Teacher Specialist—History/Social Studies
Office of Curriculum & Instruction
Norfolk Public Schools

Publishing Credits

Rachelle Cracchiolo, M.S.Ed., *Publisher*
Conni Medina, M.A.Ed., *Editor in Chief*
Emily R. Smith, M.A.Ed., *Content Director*
Véronique Bos, *Creative Director*
Robin Erickson, *Art Director*
Michelle Jovin, M.A., *Associate Editor*
Kevin Panter, *Senior Graphic Designer*

Image Credits: front cover (left), p.1, p.6 (right), p.19 (top r), p.26 (r) Franklin D. Roosevelt Library & Museum; front cover (top r), p.1 FPG/Getty Images; front cover (center r), p.1 Design Pics Inc/Alamy; front cover (bottom r), p.1, p.7, p.8, p.9 (all), p.10 (all), p.11, p.12 (top), p.13 (top r), p.17 (l), p.22 (all), p.24 (l), p.25 (top r), p.25 (bottom), p.27 (top r), p.27 (bottom), p.29 (top), p.32 U.S. National Archives; pp.2–3 LOC [LC-DIG-hec-47304]; p.4 Marine Corps Archives & Special Collections; pp.4–5 (bottom) Sueddeutsche Zeitung Photo/Alamy; p.5 (top) LOC [LC-DIG-ppmsca-1917]; p.5 (r) LOC [LC-DIG-ppmsca-35645]; p.13 (l), p.19 (top l) Everett Collection Historical/Alamy; p.14 (l) The Illustrated London News, May 15, 1915 [p.631]; pp.14–15, p.15 Naval History and Heritage Command; p.14 (bottom) LOC [LC-USZ62-93456]; p.16 David J. & Janice L. Frent Collection/Corbis/Getty Images; p.18 (l) Hulton Archive/Getty Images; pp.18–19 Bettman/Getty Images; p.19 (bottom), p.24 (r) Everett Historical/Shutterstock; p.20 (r) courtesy Lejeune Collection; pp.20–21 Keystone/Getty Images; p.21 (top) John Frost Newspapers/Alamy; p.21 (r) Florida Department of Corrections; p.23 (l) LOC [LC-USF33-T01-001398-M4]; p.25 (top l) LOC [LC-USE6-D-008362]; p.27 (top l) Galerie Bilderwelt/Getty Images; p.29 (bottom) Library of Congress [LC-DIG-hec-47244]; all other images from iStock and/or Shutterstock.

Library of Congress Cataloging-in-Publication Data
Names: Greathouse, Lisa E., author.
Title: Franklin D. Roosevelt : a great leader in troubled times / Lisa Perlman Greathouse.
Description: Huntington Beach, CA : Teacher Created Materials, [2020] | Includes index. | Audience: Ages 7 | Audience: Grades 2-3 | Summary: "As the 32nd president of the United States, Franklin Delano Roosevelt tackled some of the toughest times the United States has ever seen. His leadership lifted the country out of the Great Depression and through World War II. And he did it all while facing serious personal obstacles. It is why he is remembered for being one of the most compassionate and courageous leaders of all time."-- Provided by publisher.
Identifiers: LCCN 2019024318 (print) | LCCN 2019024319 (ebook) | ISBN 9781425850692 (paperback) | ISBN 9781425850692 (ebook)
Subjects: LCSH: Roosevelt, Franklin D. (Franklin Delano), 1882-1945--Juvenile literature. | Presidents--United States--Biography--Juvenile literature. | United States--Politics and government--1933-1945--Juvenile literature. | People with disabilities--United States--Biography--Juvenile literature. | Hyde Park (Dutchess County, N.Y.)--Biography--Juvenile literature.
Classification: LCC E807 .G693 2020 (print) | LCC E807 (ebook) | DDC 973.917092 [B]--dc23
LC record available at https://lccn.loc.gov/2019024318
LC ebook record available at https://lccn.loc.gov/2019024319

TCM Teacher Created Materials
5301 Oceanus Drive
Huntington Beach, CA 92649-1030
www.tcmpub.com
ISBN 978-1-4258-5069-2

Table of Contents

A Strong Leader

Franklin Delano Roosevelt became president of the United States in 1933. At that time, the nation was in deep trouble. Millions of people were out of work. Businesses and banks had closed. Many families had lost their homes and were living on the streets. People could not afford to buy food. This time was known as the **Great Depression**. It was one of the most difficult periods in U.S. history. However Roosevelt—called FDR for short—was up to the challenge. He found solutions to the nation's problems. Roosevelt also offered words of comfort, which gave Americans hope for the future.

A few years later, FDR faced a new crisis—World War II. The American people had complete faith in FDR. Under FDR's leadership, the United States survived the war and came out even stronger. Roosevelt did it all while facing serious health problems that left him unable to walk. His determination and strength helped make him one of the nation's most admired presidents.

U.S. troops during World War II ▼

FDR in 1933 ▲

Farmers ask for help in 1933. ▲

A Presidential Record

FDR was elected president of the United States four times! That's a record that will never be broken. In 1951, the Twenty-Second **Amendment** was added to the U.S. Constitution. It states that no president may serve more than two terms.

My Cousin, the President

FDR wasn't the first Roosevelt at the White House. His fifth cousin, Theodore (shown above), was named vice president in 1900. The next year, President William McKinley was shot and killed. Theodore ("Teddy") Roosevelt became president. Even though the two men shared a last name, Teddy was actually a closer relation to FDR's wife, Eleanor. She was Teddy's niece!

Early Years

Franklin Delano Roosevelt was born in Hyde Park, New York, on January 30, 1882. His parents were Sara and James Roosevelt. The Roosevelts came from a long line of wealthy families in the Hudson Valley and lived in a big house called Springwood. Sara was 27 years old when FDR was born; James was almost twice her age. "At quarter to nine my Sallie [Sara] had a splendid large baby boy. He weighs 10 lbs. [pounds], without clothes," James wrote the day FDR was born.

Learning at Home

FDR didn't go to public school. Instead, his mother taught him how to read and write. Private teachers taught him languages, mathematics, science, and history. Roosevelt was an only child, and his mother worried about him. So, FDR didn't often get to play with children his own age.

A Hobby That "Stuck"

As a child, FDR collected stamps. He enjoyed this hobby so much, he continued collecting stamps all his life—even after he became president. Every week, the State Department would send him unique stamps they found on letters sent to the president. Roosevelt would add them to his collection.

FDR and his mother in 1887

FDR (leaning on his grandfather's wheelchair) and his 12 cousins

Both parents adored their only child. James took FDR sledding and rowing on the Hudson River. James also taught his son how to ride a horse and how to hunt. At the family's summer home in Maine, FDR learned how to sail his father's **yacht**. Even though the family's large home and farm were tended by hundreds of workers, James taught FDR the value of hard work and the importance of helping others who were less fortunate. Roosevelt never forgot these lessons.

Going to Groton

Even though FDR did not often have the chance to play with other kids, he did see a lot of the world. As a child, he and his parents traveled through Europe. He met people from different cultures and learned from them. Roosevelt was comfortable talking to people from all backgrounds. He had a charm that would serve him well during his political career.

When FDR turned 14, his parents sent him to a **boarding school** in Groton, Massachusetts. Sara wrote in her journal that day about the sadness she and James felt at FDR leaving. She wrote, "James and I feel this parting very much, it is hard to leave my darling boy."

FDR (front row, second from the left) and the Groton football team

FDR in a school play at Groton in 1900

Growing Up

Roosevelt was 14 years old when he arrived at Groton. He was relatively small, with a height of 5 feet 3 inches (1.6 meters). By the time he graduated four years later, he had grown to 6 feet 1 inch (1.85 meters)!

Visiting Hyde Park

FDR's childhood home in Hyde Park, New York, is now a National Historic Site. Guests can tour the house, rose gardens, and gravesite where FDR and his wife are buried. Also on the site is the FDR Presidential Library and Museum.

FDR earned good grades. However, it wasn't always easy for him to fit in with the other young men. Most of the other students had attended Groton School for a couple of years. They all knew each other well. Roosevelt decided to get involved in school activities. He worked as the manager for the baseball team. He played football and acted in the theater group as well. Roosevelt wasn't always the best, but he tried hard and won over his classmates with his positive attitude and clever ideas.

Life at Harvard

FDR graduated from Groton in 1900. He then went to Harvard University. A few months after FDR got there, his father died of **heart failure**. Roosevelt was heartbroken. He was very close with his father. However FDR continued his studies, just as his parents had wished.

FDR did not get good grades during his college years. This was a normal practice at the time for children from wealthy families. Many wealthy children **aspired** to earn a "gentleman's C." Grades were not as important then. Instead, meeting people and making social connections were the main priorities in college. Roosevelt played sports and joined clubs during his time at Harvard. He also became the editor of the school newspaper, the *Harvard Crimson*, during his senior year. In 1903, FDR graduated from Harvard.

Eleanor's Life

Eleanor never felt like she fit in. When she was young, her mother teased her about her plain looks and shyness. By the time Eleanor was 10 years old, both her parents and one brother had died. On her wedding day, Eleanor's Uncle Teddy walked her down the aisle. Teddy had been sworn in for his second term as president just two weeks before the wedding.

A Passion to Help

Even though Eleanor grew up in a wealthy family, she cared about helping less-fortunate people. She volunteered in poor schools and tried to improve working conditions for women and girls. Eleanor and FDR's desire to help people was one of the things that brought them together.

FDR (front center) with the *Harvard Crimson* staff

FDR's graduation wasn't the only important **milestone** in 1903. That same year, FDR asked a woman named Eleanor to marry him. The two had met at parties and dances over the years and had grown close. Sara thought they were too young to wed. So, the couple waited two years and married in 1905.

Eleanor and FDR in 1906

FDR shakes hands with potential voters in 1910.

Entering Politics

FDR went to Columbia Law School next. Two years later, FDR passed the **bar exam** and left school. He then worked at a New York City law firm for a few years. However, he soon realized that it wasn't the right fit for him. Roosevelt wanted to be a leader more than a lawyer.

In 1910, Roosevelt ran as a Democrat for a seat in the New York State Senate. He had a famous last name and enough money for his campaign. However, most of the voters in the **rural** district (which included FDR's home in Hyde Park) were Republican. So FDR came up with a fresh idea; he drove around in a bright red car, meeting people face-to-face. Roosevelt told voters he would work toward creating an honest government. He said he would help working-class citizens. On Election Day, the 28-year-old FDR won by 1,440 votes. Roosevelt made a name for himself by fighting **corruption**, just as he had promised. He was elected to a second term in 1912.

FDR works as a New York state senator in 1911.

A Growing Family

Soon after the Roosevelts were married, they became parents. Their daughter Anna was born in 1906. The couple had five more children after Anna. Sadly, one of their children—Franklin Jr.—died from the flu before his first birthday.

It's Complicated

FDR's mother and wife had a complicated relationship. Early on, they were very close. Eleanor's mother had died when Eleanor was young. Eleanor trusted Sara's advice. However, Sara did not like how Eleanor raised her children. The relationship between the two women changed many times throughout their lives.

A Perfect Fit

In 1912, FDR helped Woodrow Wilson campaign for president. When Wilson won, he asked FDR to serve as assistant secretary for the U.S. Navy. Roosevelt had never served in the navy. However, he loved sailing. Roosevelt thought this was the perfect job for him. It was also one of Teddy Roosevelt's jobs before he became president. That interested FDR. He left the state senate and accepted Wilson's offer. Roosevelt visited **naval bases** around the country. His ideas earned him the respect of many naval leaders. Roosevelt had this job for seven years.

Eleanor's Expanding Role

While FDR helped guide the country through World War I, Eleanor was helping on the home front. She volunteered for the Red Cross and the Navy-Marine Corps Relief Society. In the years following the war, she joined the League of Women Voters. Soon, she was more popular than her husband!

Joining the War

In 1915, Germany attacked a British ship called the *Lusitania*. Half the people on the ship died, including 128 Americans. People were angry. Still, President Wilson stayed out of the war. Two years later, Wilson learned that Germany had promised U.S. land to Mexico after the war. That was the tipping point, and the United States joined the war.

FDR in 1913 ▲

The World at War

In 1914, World War I began in Europe. Roosevelt wanted the United States to join the Allies in the fight against Germany and the Axis powers. He encouraged naval leaders to build large battleships. However, President Wilson wanted to stay out of the war. Over the next few years, the relationship between the United States and Germany worsened. In 1917, the United States declared war on Germany. Roosevelt took an active part in his role with the navy. In 1918, the United States and the Allies won the war against the Axis powers.

FDR inspects the U.S. Navy's weapons in France.

A Vice Presidential Loss

Roosevelt returned to private life after the war. Yet, he did not stay out of the public eye for long. In 1919, leaders of the Democratic Party asked FDR to run for vice president. He accepted the nomination. However, the Democratic candidate for president—James Cox—lost the election to Republican Warren G. Harding. With a Republican in the White House, FDR left Washington, DC, and went into private business. Still, he never gave up his dream of higher political office.

Roosevelt family in 1920

Were They Wrong?

For years, FDR's polio diagnosis was taken as fact. But in 2003, a group of scientists at the University of Texas made a shocking announcement. They believe FDR may have suffered from Guillain-Barré syndrome. That is a rare disease that causes muscle weakness. If they are correct, it could be one of the worst misdiagnoses of all time.

A Personal Challenge

In 1921, the Roosevelts were spending time at their summer home in Canada. After swimming with his children, FDR became ill. At first, he thought it was the flu. He went upstairs to rest. Those would be some of the last steps he would ever take on his own. Doctors told FDR he had **polio**. Roosevelt wasn't sure he could have a political career if he had to spend the rest of his life in a wheelchair. He was just 39 years old. Roosevelt feared his political dreams were over.

Whose Face Is on the Dime?

In 1938, FDR started the March of Dimes to raise money for polio research. He asked everyone in the nation to mail in one dime. Roosevelt's portrait was put on the coin in 1946 to honor his work for the organization.

Back to Politics

FDR never recovered the full use of his legs and spent much of the rest of his life in a wheelchair. He wore leg braces and leaned on podiums while giving speeches. Roosevelt did not try to hide his condition from the public. However, he did not speak freely about it either. Roosevelt asked for privacy and requested that his photo not be taken while he was getting into or out of his wheelchair.

Doing it Himself

Roosevelt did not like any of his wheelchairs, so he designed his own. He used a kitchen table chair, bicycle and tricycle tires, and a set of braces on his feet and lower body that kept his legs straight. The braces made it possible for FDR to stand up with the help of crutches or a cane.

Hoovervilles

During the Great Depression, up to 15 million Americans were without jobs. Millions of people were homeless. Some of these people built towns filled with cardboard houses. These camps were nicknamed Hoovervilles, after the president at the time, Herbert Hoover. Many people blamed him for their hardships.

▼ Hooverville in Seattle, Washington

Despite his health challenges, FDR ran for governor of New York in 1928. He won the election after a close vote. The following year, in October, the **stock market** crashed, and the Great Depression began. Banks closed overnight. Business owners shut their doors, and people lost their jobs. People who had invested their money in the stock market lost everything. They lost their homes and were forced to live on the streets. Hungry people lined up in “breadlines” for meals.

▲ People wait in a breadline during the Great Depression.

New Deal

The Great Depression kept getting worse. Roosevelt knew people were hurting and tried to help. As governor, he started programs to help needy families. He asked businesses to change their schedules to keep more people employed year-round. Roosevelt easily won the election to a second term. His reputation as a fighter spread across the country. Roosevelt began to think about what he could do next.

As the 1932 presidential race neared, it was clear that people wanted a president who would fight for them. Roosevelt traveled across the country meeting voters. He had ideas about how to get people back to work. Roosevelt compared his plans to a card game, saying he wanted to give everyone a new set of cards. He called it the "New Deal."

Not everyone agreed with FDR's ideas. Many Republicans did not like the government getting involved in people's lives. They thought FDR was blaming the wealthy for the Great Depression. Even some Democrats tried to find a different candidate. In the end, Roosevelt won the Democratic nomination for president. He went on to crush President Hoover in the election. Roosevelt called it the "greatest night of my life."

Omaha World-Herald
Morning

ROOSEVELT SWEEPS NATION

SEE ROOSEVELT WINNING COUNTY BY 25,000 VOTES

Bryan Is an Easy Victor Over Griswold.

A CLEAN SWEEP

ALL NEBRASKA TICKET GOING TO DEMOCRATS

Roosevelt Assumes a Commanding Lead in State.

Nebraska Winners

DEFEAT IS CONCEDED IN HOOVER'S WIRE

President Leading in 6 States Only, with Governor's Electoral Vote Standing at 472, with Probability of Increasing to a Record Total.

BOTH HOUSE AND SENATE APPEAR TO BE STRONGLY DEMOCRATIC

DEMOCRATS CAPTURE ALL POTTAWATTAMIE

Courthouse Is Swept; Veterans Fall in Sweep.

LIQUOR PROSECUTION MAY REST CASE TODAY

Towl and Wheeler Testify to Actions of Police Officers.

HOOVER DISPATCHES

ROOSEVELT IN HIGH SPIRITS AT HIS HOME

Still Has No Comment of Message from Hoover.

Fear Itself

On March 4, 1933, FDR gave his first **inaugural address**. He gave people hope with the now-famous words: "The only thing we have to fear is fear itself." He was telling people to have courage as they worked to fix the economy.

▼ FDR delivers his first inaugural address.

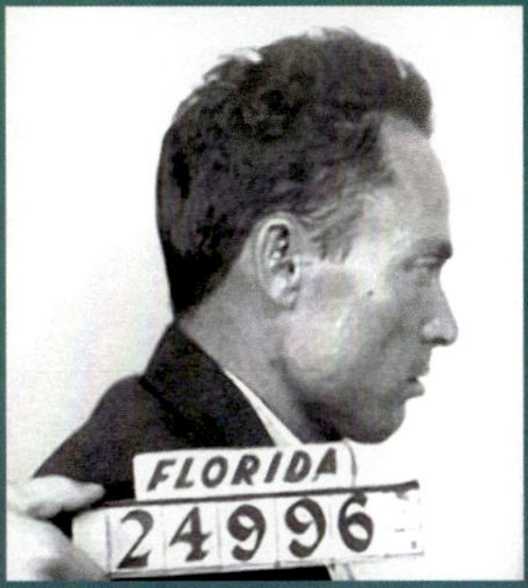

A Brush with Death

In February 1933, FDR was in Florida giving a speech. A man named Giuseppe Zangara shouted, "Too many people are starving!" and fired six shots at FDR's car. Roosevelt was not hurt, but other people were. One of the victims, the Chicago mayor, died from his injuries.

Fireside Chats

FDR spoke on the radio a few days after taking office. He explained to Americans how his new plans would help them. No president had ever spoken directly to Americans like this before. People liked these "fireside chats." Roosevelt gave around 30 more fireside chats while president.

A Sense of Security

One part of the New Deal was the Social Security Act of 1935. This act is still around. It sets aside money for people who are over 65 years old. Today, 9 out of 10 **eligible** Americans receive money from Social Security.

▲ A crowd of people tries to withdraw money from a bank in 1932.

The Hundred Days

Once FDR took office, he made good on his promises. Roosevelt worked with Congress to put his New Deal plan into action. The first thing he needed to do was to convince people to trust banks again. Most banks had closed. People were quickly taking their money out of the banks that were still open. Two days after taking office, FDR temporarily closed all banks in a move he called a "bank holiday." During this time, federal officials decided which banks were **stable** enough to re-open. After this, people felt much safer about putting their money in banks.

The banking crisis wasn't the only thing FDR was working on. Roosevelt also started programs to put young men back to work. Some of the new jobs helped communities. Young people were hired to plant trees, build hospitals, and fight forest fires, among other jobs. Not all of FDR's programs worked. However, Americans felt better knowing he was trying to turn things around. Slowly, the country began to recover.

▼ Young men work in one of FDR's New Deal programs.

Growing Trouble

Roosevelt was focused on fixing the United States' problems. Elsewhere, tensions were growing between countries. In Germany, Adolf Hitler and his Nazi Party had risen to power. They were threatening to take control of nearby countries. In 1939, German soldiers invaded Poland. Leaders of other countries rushed to take sides. World War II had begun.

Many people in the United States did not want to join the war. In 1940, FDR won a historic third term as president. He said he would keep the United States out of the war. The country's position changed one year later. On December 7, 1941, Japanese pilots bombed the U.S. naval base at Pearl Harbor, Hawai'i. The attack killed about 2,500 Americans. Most of the Pacific **fleet** was destroyed. The next day, Congress granted FDR's request to go to war with Japan. Three days later, leaders from Germany and Italy declared war on the United States.

▼ A Japanese bomber attacks Pearl Harbor.

◀ FDR signs the declaration of war against Japan on December 8, 1941.

Americans answered FDR's call-to-arms. Young men joined the military. At home, people **rationed** food and goods to help the war effort. Women got jobs, which helped fuel the economy. The nation was soon lifted out of the Great Depression.

Workers assemble a warplane during World War II.

A young boy buys juice with his ration book in 1943.

Working Women

Rosie the Riveter is a symbol of women's rights. During World War II, the U.S. government used images like Rosie to encourage women to join the workforce. Rosie appeared on posters and on TV. There was even a wartime song called "Rosie the Riveter."

Eleanor's Work

As First Lady, Eleanor toured the country. She helped people who were struggling to find work. During the war, she visited American military members both at home and overseas. All four of her sons were in the military. So she knew how important these visits were to members of the military and their families.

FDR's Funeral

Thousands of people lined the streets during FDR's funeral. Leaders of many countries went to the service. British Prime Minister Winston Churchill was FDR's close friend. Churchill cried when he told the British people about FDR's death.

United Nations

During World War II, a group of nations agreed to fight together. Roosevelt called this group the United Nations. When the war ended, leaders from 50 nations joined the UN. Sadly, FDR died before this happened. Eleanor, though, served as the chairman of the Human Rights Commission. She helped draft the Universal Declaration of Human Rights. This document lists rights that all people should have. It is seen as one of the most important milestones in UN history.

This photograph of FDR was taken one day before he died.

FDR's Last Days

By early 1945, the war was almost over. Roosevelt had been elected to a fourth term. But the stress of the job had taken a toll on his health. In March, FDR spoke to Congress while seated instead of leaning against the podium like he normally did. He told Congress that he felt "refreshed and inspired" and downplayed his health concerns.

On April 12, 1945, FDR died of a brain **hemorrhage**. He was 63 years old. Less than a month later, Germany surrendered. The war in Europe was over. Millions of Americans **mourned** the loss of the leader who had lifted them out of such hard times. He was buried in the garden of his family home in Hyde Park.

▲ A crowd salutes as FDR's coffin goes past.

Eleanor's Last Days

After FDR's death, Eleanor Roosevelt was asked to serve as U.S. representative to the newly formed United Nations (UN). She worked for the UN for seven years. Even after she left, she spent the rest of her life continuing to fight for human rights. Eleanor Roosevelt died in 1962. She was buried beside her husband. Both Franklin and Eleanor are remembered as two of the world's most admired leaders.

Eleanor Roosevelt at a UN meeting in 1947 ▼

Journal It!

Imagine that you are FDR in December 1941. The U.S. economy is slowly improving while a war rages in Europe. Until now, you have tried to keep the United States out of the war. Suddenly, Americans are attacked at Pearl Harbor, and you know you have to act.

Write two journal entries from FDR's perspective. The first entry should be written on December 6, 1941. You may want to write about the progress of the New Deal or people you met that day. Then, write a second entry on December 7, 1941. Your priorities are much different from what they were yesterday. Write about the attack on Pearl Harbor and how you feel about the United States entering the war. You may want to reflect on what you saw during World War I. Share your journal entries with friends.

File "diary material"

March 5, 1933.

Attended St. Thomas' Church with entire family, returning in time for luncheon with family and friends.

Secretary of the Treasury in conference with Bankers and Officials all morning. Two-thirty P.M. meeting in Oval Room with all members of Cabinet, Vice-President and Speaker Rainey, outlining banking situation. Unanimous approval for Special Session of Congress Thursday, March ninth. Proclamation for this prepared and sent. This was followed by conferences with Senator Glass, Hiram Johnson, Joe Robinson and Congressmen Steagall and Byrns and Minority Leader Snell -- all in accord. Secretary Woodin reported bankers' representatives much at sea as to what to do.

Concluded that forty-eight different methods of handling banking situation impossible. Attorney General Cummings reported favorably on power to act under 1917 law, giving President power to license, regulate, etc., export, hoarding, ear-marking of gold or currency.

Based on this opinion and on emergency, deci
on Proclamation declaring banking holi
through Thursday, March nint
regulate parti

Glossary

amendment—a change to the words or meaning of a law or document

aspired—worked to get something

bar exam—a test that a person must pass to practice law in a certain area

boarding school—a school where most students live while studying

corruption—dishonest or immoral behaviors and actions

eligible—qualified to participate or to be chosen

fleet—a group of warships under one management

Great Depression—a period of time from 1929 to 1939 when many people did not have jobs and there was little money

heart failure—a condition in which a person's heart is unable to pump blood at a normal speed or amount

hemorrhage—a major loss of blood from the blood vessels

inaugural address—a speech given by a person who is newly elected to an office

milestone—an important development

mourned—expressed or felt sadness and grief

naval bases—places where navies keep supplies and from which they launch operations

polio—an infectious disease that can cause loss of movement in a person's body and the wasting away of muscles

rationed—used things carefully so as not to use too much

rural—relating to a countryside area instead of a city

stable—not likely to change or not easily changed

stock market—a system for buying and selling ownership in some companies

yacht—a small ship that is usually used for personal use

Index

Your Turn!

During his presidency, FDR gave around 30 fireside chats. These radio broadcasts ranged in time, with the longest speech lasting for 45 minutes. More than half of all adults in the United States regularly tuned in to hear FDR's chats.

This letter was written one day after the first fireside chat. In it, the listener thanks FDR for explaining in "plain and forceful language…how he was tackling the job I and my fellow citizens gave him." He asks FDR to continue these radio broadcasts and offers his appreciation to the president.

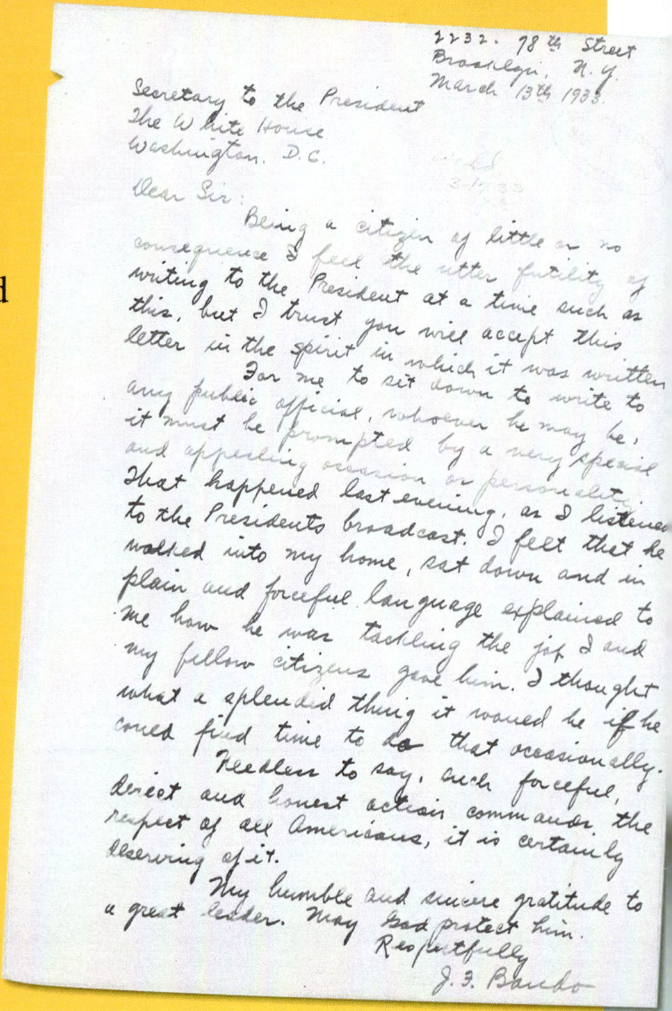

2232. 78th Street
Brooklyn, N.Y.
March 13th 1933.

Secretary to the President
The White House
Washington. D.C.

Dear Sir:

Being a citizen of little or no consequence I feel the utter futility of writing to the President at a time such as this, but I trust you will accept this letter in the spirit in which it was written.

For me to sit down to write to any public official, whoever he may be, it must be prompted by a very special and appealing occasion or personality. That happened last evening, as I listened to the Presidents broadcast. I felt that he walked into my home, sat down and in plain and forceful language explained to me how he was tackling the job I and my fellow citizens gave him. I thought what a splendid thing it would be if he could find time to do that occasionally.

Needless to say, such forceful, direct and honest action commands the respect of all Americans, it is certainly deserving of it.

My humble and sincere gratitude to a great leader. May God protect him.

Respectfully
J. J. Bancko

Think of a leader you know. It can be a mayor, a teacher, a community leader, or someone else. What have they done that you want to thank them for? What would you like to see them continue doing? Send a letter or email to that person thanking them for a job well done.